All About Animals
Birds

By Edward S. Barnard

Reader's Digest Young Families

Contents

Chapter 1
A Tale of Terns 5

Chapter 2
The Body of a Bird 13

Chapter 3
Perching Birds 23

Chapter 4
Birds of Prey 29

Chapter 5
Waterbirds 37

Glossary
Wild Words 42

Index 44

Credits 45

Chapter 1
A Tale of Terns

Terns Take Turns

A female common tern lays two or three eggs in late May. Then she and her mate take turns sitting on the eggs until they hatch—in 23 days.

A male common tern comes in for a landing near his nesting mate. The pair are living on an island with thousands of other tern pairs.

It is early June along the northeastern coast of the United States. A flock of seabirds called common terns are noisily hovering over the ocean near a small island. The terns are gray and white with forked tails, black-capped heads, and bright red beaks and feet.

A school of fish swims close to the ocean's surface, their shiny sides sparkling in the sun. Some of the terns dive headfirst into the water and quickly surface holding wiggly fish in their beaks. They shake the water from their feathers and take off into the sky, heading for the nearby island.

A male tern, his gray-tipped wing feathers spread wide, lands near a female tern sitting on a nest in a hollow place on the ground. She has two tan, speckled eggs underneath her. She is hungry and quickly swallows the fish her mate offers her as they exchange places on the nest.

Dinnertime!

Most of the time, common terns catch fish for their young. But tern parents also feed their little ones insects, shrimp, and small crabs.

Now it is mid-June, and a tiny, fluffy baby bird (called a chick) pecks its way out of one of the eggs in the nest. A day later a second chick struggles out of the other egg. The female tern squats over the chicks, shading them from the hot sun. The male tern flies in from the ocean with a fish and tries to feed it to one of the chicks. The fish looks almost as big as the chick! It dangles from the chick's mouth for a minute or so but finally disappears. Both parents look for food and feed the chicks. The male tern brings in more fish for the chicks than the female does.

The tern colony is a very noisy place during daylight hours. Hundreds of terns swoop and circle in the sky over the island, calling out *ter-arr* and making a rapid *kip-kip-kip* sound. Sometimes a few gulls fly close to the island, hoping to carry off a tern chick or two. Then hundreds of shrieking terns angrily take to the air and chase the gulls away.

Weighed and Measured

Scientists study terns on Great Gull Island, near New York City. They weigh the birds, measure their beaks, and put tiny numbered bands on their legs. When a banded bird is caught again, sometimes years later in another place, the band will show scientists where the bird came from.

A newly born common tern chick grows fast. After a week it may weigh three times as much as it did when it hatched.

This young common tern, standing next to a parent, is about 24 days old. Its wing feathers are not fully grown.

As the tern chicks grow, new and larger feathers replace their down, or tiny fluffy feathers. Gray and brown feathers sprout on their wings. Black feathers cover their heads. When people walk by the nest, the young birds scurry into nearby weeds while their parents dive close to the human intruders. Anyone who forgets to wear a hat is likely to receive painful pecks on the head!

Once the young terns grow wing feathers, they try to fly, running along the ground and flapping their wings. By the time they are three to four weeks old, they take to the air for short flights. Their parents still bring them fish, sometimes feeding them in midair. In another week or two, the young terns will fly longer distances on fishing expeditions, and their parents will stop feeding them. They must then take care of themselves.

As summer ends, thousands of young terns gather in flocks. Soon they will leave the island and fly more than 4,000 miles to South America. They will live along the coast of Brazil or Argentina for two years and then return to the island where they were born to raise their own families.

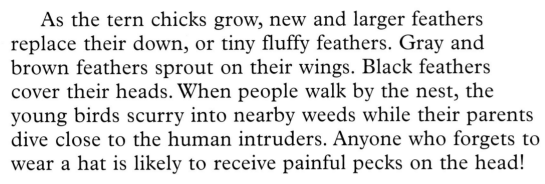

Ready to Take Off

This young tern is learning to fly. Scientists on Great Gull Island call birds at this stage "Orvilles," after Orville Wright, one of the inventors of the airplane.

Chapter 2
The Body of a Bird

The male peafowl, also called a peacock, fans out his iridescent feathers to impress peahens, the females. Peahens have plainer, shorter feathers.

Feathers and Bones

Birds are the only animals with feathers. They need feathers to help maintain their body heat. Birds are warm-blooded, which means their body temperature always stays the same. Feathers also make it possible for birds to fly. Without wing and tail feathers, birds couldn't get off the ground. In addition, feathers give birds color—for camouflage and for attracting mates. A plucked bird looks completely different from a feathered one!

Birds are descended from reptiles, and their feathers developed from reptilian scales. Birds still have scales on their legs.

Birds have very lightweight bones, which are usually hollow and air-filled. A bird's bones, in fact, can be lighter than all of its feathers.

Light and Flexible

A bird that is a strong flier or swimmer has a large breastbone beneath its chest. The breastbone holds the big muscles powering the bird's wings.

A bird has more separate bones in its neck than a human has and can turn its head to face backward.

15

Wings and Feet

Every bird has wings, even a bird that can't fly, such as a penguin. A bird's wing is curved so that both the thicker leading edge and the thinner trailing edge are lower than the middle of the wing. This curved shape helps to give the wing "lift." As a bird flaps its wings, its feathers twist to let air through on the upstroke and flatten to catch more air on the downstroke.

The shape of a bird's wings is different depending on the bird's way of life. The fastest bird is the peregrine falcon. Its sweptback, streamlined wings allow it to dive for prey at more than 175 miles per hour! Vultures have broad, rounded wings that let them hover in the air as they scan the ground below for food. Birds that don't fly much, such as pheasants, have short, stubby wings.

Feet with a Difference

Feet tell a lot about how birds live. Many waterbirds that swim have webbed feet. Most perching birds have back toes that wrap around tree limbs. Eagles have muscular toes and sharp nails for clutching prey.

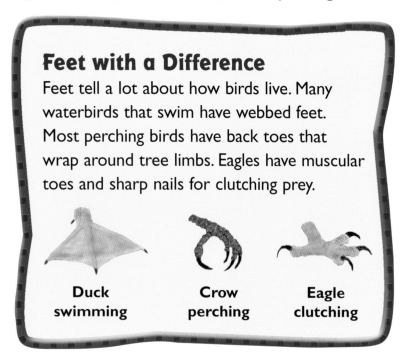

Duck swimming **Crow perching** **Eagle clutching**

Flying Lesson

LOW PRESSURE

HIGH PRESSURE

Lift ↑

The pressure of air flowing under a bird's wings is greater than the pressure of air above them. The pressure from below pushes (lifts) the wings up.

As a great egret flaps its wings, the wing feathers fan out to catch the air. The bird's long legs and long, thin toes allow it to wade in water and walk on mud.

Toucans, birds of the tropical rain forests, have large but lightweight bills. The bills are perfect for picking fruits, attracting mates, and fighting with rivals.

Beaks and Eyes

Birds don't have teeth. Instead, they have hard, bony beaks, which are also called bills. The shape of a bird's beak depends usually on what the bird eats. Eagles and owls have hooked beaks that can grab and tear up prey. Spoonbills have long, flattened bills that they swing slowly back and forth in water to strain out tiny animals and plants. Woodpeckers have sharp beaks for digging holes into trees to reach burrowing insects.

Woodpecker

Spoonbill

Some birds have eyes on the sides of their heads, allowing them to see predators approaching from almost any direction. The eyes of birds of prey are in the front of

their heads. This position helps them judge distances accurately. Some birds can see detail and color better than humans. Golden eagles can spot hares that are a mile away! Hummingbirds can see small red flowers from half a mile off.

Big Bird and Little Bird

Like other birds, ostriches have feathers, wings, beaks, and two legs. The females lay eggs. Unlike most other birds, however, they can't fly, even though they have wings. Penguins also can't fly, but they use their wings to swim.

Ostriches are the heaviest, tallest, and fastest-running birds. They can weigh up to 350 pounds—the weight of two good-sized men. They reach 9 feet in height—taller than the tallest basketball player. They can run more than 40 miles an hour—as fast as the fastest racehorse. They lay the world's heaviest eggs—each one weighs as much as 24 chicken eggs!

The smallest bird is the bee hummingbird of Cuba. It is only two and a half inches long—about the length of an adult's little finger. It weighs less than a penny and lays pea-sized eggs.

Sweet Snack

Hummingbirds feed on the nectar, or sweet liquid, in flowers. They eat more than their weight in food every day. They are the only birds that can hover for long periods and fly backward or straight up!

Ostriches live in groups of 100 or more. They can't fly with their wings, but they do use them for balance when they run and for waving to attract mates.

Chapter 3
Perching Birds

The cardinal probably deserves the title of America's most popular songbird. Seven states have named it their official state bird! Unlike many other songbirds, it does not fly south for the winter.

Biggest Bird Group

There are over 9,500 different kinds, or species, of birds in the world. More than half are in a group called perching birds. These birds have three toes facing forward and one backward. When a perching bird begins to lean backward, its feet tighten their grip so the bird can easily cling to twigs, reeds, and power lines—even when it is asleep!

Some perching birds are songbirds. They have special muscles in their throats that are used for singing. Many songbirds, such as song sparrows and warblers, make sounds that are pleasant for us to listen to. Ravens and others do little more than croak.

Songbirds sing to attract mates and to keep rivals out of their nesting grounds. They also use songs to signal danger and tell others about new feeding places. Chicks use songs to tell parents they are hungry.

Fewer Bluebirds

Like the cardinal, the bluebird is a beautiful and popular songbird, but its numbers are decreasing. Starlings and house sparrows compete with it for its favorite nesting spots—empty holes in old trees and fence posts.

Billions of Birds

Perching birds are the most plentiful birds on the planet. There are almost a half billion starlings and house sparrows in the United States. And pigeons live in nearly every major city of the world.

Every spring the redwinged blackbird nests in North American farmlands and wet places, such as marshes and lakeshores. Flying in large flocks, the males arrive first and announce their territories with repeated calls. A few days later the females fly in. After the redwinged pairs raise their young, they form huge flocks, sometimes numbering in the millions. Farmers are not happy when the flocks settle in fields and damage crops.

Hungry Hordes

The red-billed quelea of Africa is the world's most numerous bird. There are over one and a half billion of them! When millions of queleas settle on farms, they can cause serious crop damage.

This flock of redwinged blackbirds and yellow-headed blackbirds built their nests in a large marsh. The redwingeds nested around the edges of the marsh and the yellow heads nested in the center.

Chapter 4
Birds of Prey

To cut down on wind resistance, an osprey carries the fish it has just caught headfirst. Barbed pads on the osprey's feet help this bird keep a firm grip on its slippery prey.

Gigantic Nests

This huge osprey nest is built on top of a cactus in California. Ospreys often use the same nest year after year, adding new sticks each season. A big nest can weigh 1,000 pounds or more!

Eagles and Hawks

A bird of prey hunts by using the sharp claws, called talons, on its muscular feet to catch fish, mice, rabbits, and other birds. Eagles are large, powerful birds of prey with keen eyesight, hooked beaks for tearing flesh, and broad wings for fast flight. One of the best-known eagles is the white-headed American bald eagle. It eats fish and usually lives near water.

Hawks are medium-sized birds of prey. Some have longer tails and shorter wings than eagles. Other hawks, such as the red-tailed hawk, have long, wide wings. They can soar for hours, seldom flapping their wings.

The osprey lives on every continent in the world except Antarctica. It hunts by diving feet first into water and grabbing fish near the surface.

Fierce Hunter

The golden eagle uses its talons for killing and carrying prey. The talons are much stronger than the hands of a human being.

Hunters of the Night

Most birds of prey hunt in the daytime, but owls usually hunt at night and roost in trees during the day. They are most active just after sunset or just before sunrise. Before they begin to hunt, owls comb their head feathers with their claws. Then they take off silently on wings edged with extra-soft feathers that muffle sound.

The eyes of owls face forward like ours do, helping owls to judge distances well. Their eyes are very big compared to the size of their heads. Owls also have excellent hearing and can even pinpoint the exact location of mice under snow.

An owl often perches on a low tree branch or fence post, waiting for an animal to move. Then it swoops down silently with its talons stretched out. Often the owl hits its prey hard enough to stun it before grabbing the creature.

Day Hunter

The snowy owl lives in treeless Arctic regions. Unlike most other owls, it hunts in the daytime. Its white feathers help it blend into its surroundings.

Owls have super night vision. Their eyes are up to one hundred times more sensitive to light than ours. Together with their excellent hearing, owls can locate and catch prey in almost total darkness!

The Andean condor of South America is the world's largest bird of prey. Its wingspan is 10 ½ feet! Like other vultures, it has only a few feathers on its head because they would get dirty when it eats.

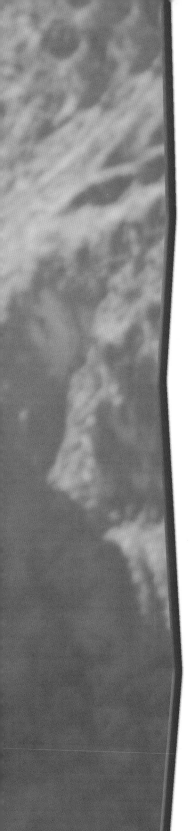

Vultures

Vultures are birds of prey that feed on dead or dying animals. They don't carry food to their young in their talons. They eat the food first and then disgorge it directly into the chicks' mouths.

Vultures are considered disgusting by many people, but they play an important role in the web of life. Without becoming sick themselves, they get rid of rotting meat that might kill other animals if they were to eat it.

Condors are the largest vultures. Males weigh up to 33 pounds. Condors live in the mountains of California and South America. While taking off, they flap their wings but then sail for hours high in the sky with hardly a flap. When they spot dead animals or other vultures already feeding, they land and rip into the hides of even the toughest carcasses.

Lord of the Vultures

The king vulture lives in the rain forests of South America. Other vultures make way for these big, aggressive birds.

Chapter 5
Waterbirds

Puffins are one of the few
birds that can hold several
fish in their beak at once!

Birds of Sea and Shore

Some seabirds, such as gannets and puffins, live out in the open ocean for many months each year. They feed on fish by diving underwater. In the spring and summer, these birds come ashore on islands where thousands of them nest close together.

Pelicans stay close to shore most of the time. They, too, dive for fish underwater. Pelicans have a stretchy pouch under the lower part of their big bill. After scooping up a fish along with a pouch full of water, the pelican comes to the ocean's surface. The water drains out of the pouch, and the pelican then swallows the fish.

Gulls stay along the shore too. They eat seafood and also almost anything else they can find—from insects, dead animals, and berries to garbage.

Keeping Dry

Sandpipers always stay just ahead of the surf as they run along the seashore. And somehow they know exactly where to stick their bill in the sand to catch a worm or small crab.

Wetland Birds

Lakes, rivers, streams, ponds, and marshes are good places to see birds. Even ponds in city parks are likely to have ducks, geese, and swans. Wet places offer birds water, food, and protection from predators.

Pond ducks, such as mallards, usually feed in the water near the shore. They snap up tiny plants floating in the water and tip over headfirst to pull up plants from the pond's muddy bottom. Swans also feed on underwater plants, stirring up the bottom by pumping their feet and stretching their heads and long necks into the water to yank up plant roots. Geese feed on land, grazing on grass and grain.

Long-legged wading birds—such as cranes, storks, and herons—stand quietly in shallow water waiting for fish or frogs to come within range of their lightning-quick, sharply pointed beaks.

Saved!

Wood ducks were once endangered because of hunting and the cutting down of their nesting trees. To help save these ducks, many people put nest boxes around woodland lakes and ponds. Now these beautiful ducks can be seen once again.

For the Birds

Many waterbirds and some of our most beautiful songbirds are in trouble because of changes in their habitats. Find out how you can help them by contacting your local Audubon society or go online to www.audubon.org, the website of the National Audubon Society.

The great blue heron feeds in shallow water, grabbing or spearing fish, frogs, crayfish, snakes, or anything else moving. It stands 4 feet tall and has a 7-foot wingspan.

Glossary of Wild Words

bird of prey   a meat-eating bird, such as an eagle, owl, or hawk, that hunts for food. Some birds of prey eat animals that are dying or are dead.

carcass   a dead animal

chick   a very young bird

disgorge   eject or expel food that has been swallowed

endangered   a species of animal or plant in danger of extinction

habitat   the natural environment where an animal or a plant lives

hatch   to be born by breaking out of an egg

hover   to stay in the air above one place

lift   air pressure that pushes a wing upward

perching birds birds with three toes facing forward and one backward that are used for gripping branches and other resting places

predator an animal that hunts and eats other animals to survive

prey an animal or animals that are hunted by other animals for food

roost to sit or rest on a branch or other place

scales overlapping flat pieces of keratin, the same material as your nails, that cover fish, reptiles, and the legs of birds

species a group of plants or animals that are the same in many ways

talons sharp claws on a bird of prey

warm-blooded having a body temperature that stays the same even when the outside temperature changes

wingspan the distance between wing tips

Index

B
bald eagle 28-29, 31
beaks 19, 31, 38, 39
birds of prey 28-35
blackbirds 26, 27
bluebird 25
bones 15

C
cardinal 24, 25
common terns 4-11
condors 34, 35
cranes 40
crow 16

D
ducks 16, 40

E
eagles 16, 19, 31
egrets 42-43
eyes 19, 31, 32, 33

F
feathers 14, 15
feet 16, 25, 30, 31
flying 14, 15, 16, 17, 30

G
geese 40
great egret 17
gulls 39

H
hawks 31
herons 40, 41
house sparrows 19, 20
hummingbird 19, 20

O
osprey 30, 31
ostriches 20, 21
owls 11, 19, 32, 33

P
peacocks 14
pelicans 2, 3, 39
penguin 16
perching birds 22-27
peregrine falcon 16
pheasants 16
pigeons 26
puffins 38

R
ravens 25
red-billed quelea 26
reptiles 15

S
sandpipers 39
seabirds 38, 39
sparrows 25, 26
songbirds 25, 41
spoonbills 12-13, 19
starlings 26
storks 40
swans 36-37, 40

T
talons 31
toucan 18

V
vultures 16, 34, 35

W
warblers 25
waterbirds 16, 36-41
wetland birds 40, 41
wings 16, 17
woodpecker 19